IMAGES
of Wales

AROUND
CAERPHILLY

David Williams, born Waunwaelod, Caerphilly, 1738, died London, 1816, and one of the most famous sons of the area. He founded the Royal Literary Fund, drafted the first constitution of the post-Revolution French republic and also shielded Benjamin Franklin from persecution. Parc Dafydd Williams next to Caerphilly Castle contains a memorial to him.

IMAGES
of Wales

AROUND
CAERPHILLY

Compiled by
Simon Eckley and Caerphilly Local History Society

TEMPUS

First published 1995, reprinted 1998
Copyright © Simon Eckley and Caerphilly Local History Society, 1995

Tempus Publishing Limited
The Mill, Brimscombe Port,
Stroud, Gloucestershire, GL5 2QG

ISBN 0 7524 0194

Typesetting and origination by
Tempus Publishing Limited
Printed in Great Britain by
Midway Clark Printing, Wiltshire

Children in Tynygraig Road, Llanbradach, *c.* 1935.

Contents

Foreword

By Glyndwr G. Jones, author of *Cronicl Caerffili*

I was born in Caerphilly in 1927. At that time it was a small town plagued by unemployment. The one bright feature of the place for us children was the weekly market held on the Twyn. Castle Street had houses, shops and public houses on both sides of the road. Many of the buildings backing on to the Castle were removed by the Marquis of Bute in the 1930s, to give a better view of the Castle. However, it was not until c. 1948 that the last building on this west side of Castle Street was removed. This was the butcher's shop of Mr Tom England, who had stubbornly refused to move. He died in 1947. Last year (1994) most of the other side of the street was razed to the ground to make way for a new shopping complex which is due to open shortly.

In 1841, as the tithe map shows, Castle Street *was* Caerphilly; there were only three buildings between Dadleudy (the Court House) and St Martin's Chapel in Cardiff Road. However, some historians believe that the medieval town of Caerphilly lay mostly along the road from the Twyn market place to the site of the old St Martin's Chapel, alongside the present church of St Martin. Both the annual fair, held on the Twyn and the ancient chapel were dedicated to St Martin.

In good times, many of the men of Caerphilly worked in the area's deep collieries. There was also work of a more permanent nature in the local locomotive and carriage repair and maintenance works, known as "The Sheds". All this industry has now gone and unemployment again sears the soul.

Surrounding, and in some cases close to, the town were a number of small farms which were usually whitewashed yearly. They dotted the hillsides and shone in the bright sunlight. Since the 1939-45 war most of these farms have disappeared, swept away by redevelopment or by the inability of the farmer to make a living.

Caerphilly has seen many changes. The Roman legions were here for a while, then "foreigners" occupied the new town when the Castle was first constructed and recently the town was host to the American Army during the Second World War. Substantial alterations continue to be made and it is to be hoped that new enterprises will be attracted to the town to replace the lost heavy industries.

It gives me great pleasure to write these few words as a foreword to this book. I would also like to congratulate Mr Simon Eckley and the Caerphilly History Society for a job well done. The book deserves success.

The illustrations depicted here show aspects of years gone by and remind us that we should never neglect the past which is the history of all of us. In the first issue of *Cronicl Caerffili* I quoted a piece from Alan Bennett's play *40 Years On*, which reads:

> "You could say that we are trying to shed the burden of the past. Shed it?
> Why must we shed it? Why not shoulder it? Memories are not shackles – they
> are garlands."

Glyndwr G. Jones.

Introduction

This book brings together a fresh selection of images covering various aspects of the history of Caerphilly and the surrounding district over the last century. It does not attempt to be a complete pictorial history of Caerphilly and the former mining villages of Llanbradach, Senghenydd and Abertridwr, for to do so would require four separate volumes of considerable thickness. Instead, I have tried to offer a themed series of snapshots of vanished lifestyles and lives, which in the mid-1990s as the rate of change and development of the area increases yet more rapidly, it is often difficult to imagine ever existing.

However, Caerphilly Castle, which is viewed in section one, has remained a constant, albeit for long a crumbling feature, of the landscape for over seven centuries. Such admirable continuity cannot be matched even by the houses and farms seen in section two or by the churches and chapels of section seven in this book. The condition of the castle and its surrounds before and after its restoration are shown in a series of photographs. Whatever the historical and aesthetic merits of the rebuilding orchestrated by the Marquis of Bute through the 1930s, the castle, complete with its water defences, remains a vivid symbol of the lengths the "English" had to go to in their efforts to subdue the rebellious Welsh hinterland.

The second chapter reminds us of both the rural nature of the Caerphilly community for several centuries following its plantation in the shadow of the castle, and also the scattered "farmstead" settlement which typified the uplands of Glamorgan and Monmouthshire in the era prior to the industrial revolution and the concerted exploitation of the subterranean wealth of South Wales.

Section three attempts to give an insight into the rapid growth of the mining industry and consequent dramatic transformation of the landscape. It also contains two views of earlier enterprises, closely linked with the former agricultural economy of Caerphilly: the Energlyn corn mill and the Castle woollen mill.

The industrial powerhouse that was created in the Rhymney Valley and throughout much of South Wales in the second half of the nineteenth century was to develop well into the 1900s, until depression and falls in the demand for coal initiated a long decline. However the legendary reputation of this society continued to grow and to be proudly disseminated long after, as evidenced by the visit of the colonial leader to Llanbradach Colliery (one of the most convenient to reach from Cardiff) on page 35. The demand generated by the collieries and their employees also led to the establishment of a plethora of subsidiary and service industries, many of which can be seen through the book.

The development of the railway system went hand in hand with that of the coalfield and was of particular importance for Caerphilly due to the siting of the Rhymney Railway's (later G.W.R.) Locomotive, Carriage and Wagon Works (the "Sheds") on the outskirts of the town. The Llanbradach Viaduct, meanwhile, albeit for a relatively short period in the early decades of this century, provided a spectacular monument to the omnipotence of the steam train. Its dismantling in 1937-38 is captured on pp. 43-44.

Sections 5 and 6 chart the development of the two main commercial thoroughfares, Castle Street and Cardiff Road and the point at which they converge - the historic market place on the Twyn. The shopping centre of Caerphilly was originally along Castle Street. As the twentieth century progressed it moved gradually to Cardiff Road but with the new retail complex in Castle Street soon to open the pendulum seems to have swung back.

The importance of religious and educational institutions is covered in chapters 7 and 8. The area was one of the cradles of non-conformity in South Wales with leading local evangelists instrumental in the establishment of chapels at Watford and Groeswen within three years of each other in the mid-eighteenth century (see pp. 76-77).

Chapter 9 – "Serving the Community" – illustrates some of the many ways in which it has been possible to help others, ranging from service in the Home Guard or Special Constabulary to the Llanbradach Chamber of Trade's Father Christmas.

Major events both in local and national history are examined in chapter 10 with, for example, photographs portraying different aspects of the National Eisteddfod of Wales which visited Caerffili in 1950.

Finally, sections 11 and 12 show the variety of clubs and forms of entertainment around Caerphilly, some of which, such as the charabanc outings and the jazz bands are now no more than memories. The quantity and, especially as regards the choirs, the quality of these societies is staggering. They were (and must continue to be so) part of the glue which bound together the community.

View over Caerphilly up the Rhymney Valley towards the Llanbradach Viaduct, 1930s.

One
The Castle

The east gateway to the inner ward, Caerphilly Castle, c. 1900. The castle had remained in ruins for centuries until in 1928 the owner of the land, the Marquis of Bute, began a restoration process which would continue until the end of the 1930s. The first activity was the removal of ivy which coated parts of the castle and in 1929 work began on the clearance of the east moat and the demolition of the buildings on the west side of Castle Street (see chapter 6).

Two views of Caerphilly Castle drawn by Henry Gastineau and engraved by W. Wallis, 1820s. The picture below shows the buildings which had been erected on the island in front of the east entrance to the castle.

Southern walls of Caerphilly Castle, 1930s, showing Nant-y-Gledyr (Castle Brook) which fed the Castle Woollen Mill. Houses on the Twyn can be seen in the background.

Castle falls, 1930s. Formerly there was a sluice gate here in the castle walls to control the height of the lake behind. The sluice to the left delivered water to the wheel of the Castle Woollen Mill.

Aerial view of the castle showing the fortress, c. 1938, after its restoration but before the demolition of the houses on Castle Street (bottom right) and the flooding of the water defences which took place in the 1950s.

Caerphilly Castle in the 1920s before its restoration.

Banquet in the Great Hall at Caerphilly Castle attended by the Marquis of Bute, 1971. In the background, centre left, facing the camera are Mr & Mrs W.J. Rose. Across the table from them is Mr Henry Simons, long serving teacher at Caerphilly "Grammar" School (1929–1964) and author of *Forty Years On* – the history of boys' secondary education in Caerphilly from 1912 to 1953. The banquet was held as part of the celebrations surrounding the 700th anniversary of the castle's construction.

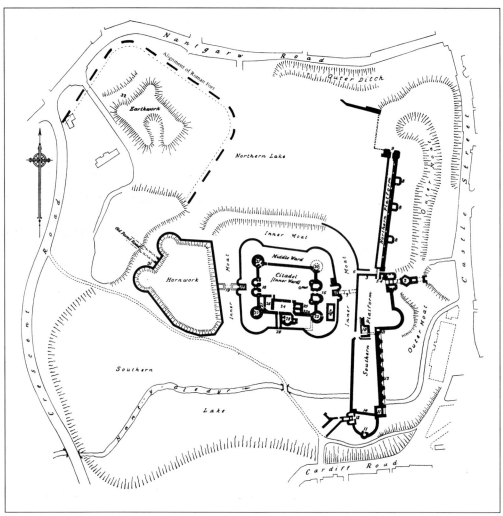

Plan of Caerphilly Castle. It is the second largest concentric castle in Britain after Windsor, covering an area of 30 acres.

CAERPHILLY CASTLE

EXPLANATORY REFERENCE.

The Eastern Front. (380–400 yds. long.)

1. Main Gateway.
2. Barbican and Double Drawbridge.
3. Cross Wall dividing Northern from Southern Platform.
4. Tower at the junction of the Northern Platform with the Main Gateway
5. Gateway between Northern and Southern Platform.
6. Outlet for water from Inner Moat controlled by Sluices.
7. Drawbridge across the Moat between the Outer and Middle Wards.
8. Chambered Bastions.
9. Gateway at the North End of the Platform.
10. Watermill with outlet for water through Curtain.
11. Mural Towers.
12. Buttresses supporting the Wall.
13. Gateway at the South End of Platform.
14. Cross Wall covering Entrance to Platform from the South.

The Citadel.

15. East Gateway to Middle Ward.
16.   ,,   ,,   ,, Inner   ,,
17. West   ,,   ,, Middle   ,,
18.   ,,   ,,   ,, Inner   ,,
19. Drawbridge across the Moat between Citadel and Hornwork.
20, 21, 22, and 23.   Drum Towers at the angles of the Inner Curtain Wall. (No. 23 The Leaning Tower.)
24. The Great Hall.
25. Buttery, etc.
25a. Chapel.
26. State Rooms.
27. Entrance to Braose Gallery.
28. Kitchen and Servants' Quarters.
29. Water Gate and Covered Passage.
30. Store House.

Hornwork.

31. Gateway with Drawbridge over the Moat.

Earthwork.

32. Moat.
33. Outer Fortification.

Aerial view of the castle, c. 1965, showing the areas on the west side of Castle Street and the north side of Cardiff Road which had been cleared in the 1930s and also the reflooded water defences. The wooded area – the redoubt – bottom left, was built as a Civil War artillery fort. In 1963 a dig conducted by Mr John Lewis of the National Museum of Wales found no traces of a medieval construction here; it had been suggested that this was the site of the original castle of Gilbert de Clare which was destroyed by Llywelyn ap Gruffydd, Prince of Wales in 1268 shortly after its completion. However, Lewis did find clear evidence of a Roman fort on the site with defences lying in the field in the bottom left corner of this photograph.

Two
Rural Life and Views Around Caerphilly

Horse parade, Caerphilly, c. 1900. This parade was part of Caerphilly's two day fair held each year on the 4 and 5 April. Horses were led through the streets of the town from the Twyn to Piccadilly Square and back again. By the beginning of this century, however, these Caerphilly fairs had lost much of their earlier importance and with some opposition from townsfolk to the movement of animals in the streets, the actual parade was transferred, c. 1908 to Virginia Park, although horse fairs continued to be held on the Twyn until well into the 1930s. The exhibition of breeding stallions, the original purpose of the event, had by now been subsumed into a more general horse show with prizes in various classes accompanied by horse racing, entertainment booths and beer tents.

Nineteenth century painting of the already unoccupied and ruined Van Mansion or Castell-y-Van. Offering a splendid view over the castle and the town, it was bought and enlarged in the early sixteenth century by Edward Lewis, a Welsh landowner, who in 1530 succeeded his father as constable of Caerphilly Castle. By the early eighteenth century the interests of the Lewis family were with property and politics elsewhere in England and Wales with St Fagan's Castle the preferred seat in the area. Part of the disused mansion was therefore turned into a farm while the remainder deteriorated into ruins. With the end of the direct male line the family estates passed in 1730 through marriage into the hands of the earls of Plymouth although minor branches of the Lewis family remained substantial landowners in other parts of South Wales.

Van Mansion, *c.* 1900.

The Van dovecote or columbarium, 1930s. This structure seems to have collapsed in the severe winter of 1947 but has now been rebuilt. A local landmark for centuries, it contained over a thousand nesting boxes and was originally used to rear doves or pigeons as a supply of fresh meat, especially during the winter, for the nearby Van Mansion.

Porch of the Van Mansion before its recent restoration.

Watford Fawr or Plas Watford, *c*. 1904. During the mid-eighteenth century the occupier of the house, Thomas Price JP was a generous supporter of the work of evangelisation carried out in the area by the Rev. David Williams and Hywel Harris. John Wesley is reputed to have stayed at Watford Fawr on several occasions. The various branches of the Price family also occupied Dadleudy (Court House) and Pontypandy House.

Pencapel Farm, above St Martin's Church, seen here in 1972, shortly before its demolition. Note the stone roof tiles.

Pontypandy House, c. 1905. This manor house, occupied until c. 1940, has now disappeared like so many of the old farms and houses in the Caerphilly area. It was demolished in the late sixties. At the time this photograph was taken the mansion had been sub-divided into three coal miners' homes. Wyndham Head sits on the bicycle, supported by his uncle George Howells.

Pontypandy Farm, c. 1930. The house is still occupied although the surrounding farmland has now disappeared in housing and retail developments. The above building was part of Pontypandy House next door and was once used as a Malthouse.

Pandy Farm, 1951. It was demolished *c.* 1972. The small ivy-clad building, top left, may have been the original pandy (fulling mill) and dye house.

Pontygwyndy Farm, 1968. It was removed in the early seventies to make way for the Carrefour hypermarket.

Hendredenny Hall (seen here in 1969) is believed to date from 1799 and was built by Rowland Williams who died in 1819. His wife, Jane, lived here until her death in 1833 and their youngest son, George, used it as a family home until the 1860s. The estate, comprising 230 acres, included the Rose and Crown public house and, from the 1860s onwards, a colliery that produced coal for twenty years.

Rear of Penyrheol-las Farm, above Energlyn, Caerphilly, 1970. Note the stone tiled roof typical of the old farms of the area.

Energlyn Farm, Caerphilly, 1956.

Tollgate cottage, situated a short distance from Porset Farm, 1956. This was demolished *c.* 1960. It was once occupied by the tollgate keeper who was responsible for the collection of tolls on this section of the old turnpike road from Caerphilly to Bedwas. There were also other tollhouses locally at Pwll-y-pant and on Wern-ddu Road between Rudry and Caerphilly.

Pwll-y-pant House, Caerphilly, 1890s. This was built about 1700 by William David, father of Rev. David Williams, the first minister at Watford Chapel, and was occupied by several generations of the family. The most illustrious of the line, was William Evan Williams who built up considerable wealth, in particular from the royalties paid by the quarries and small collieries which were opened up on his land. Eccentric to the point of madness, he bequeathed, following his death in 1870, all his not inconsiderable estate to the Marquis of Bute, hardly the neediest of recipients. Pwll-y-pant House was then subsequently occupied, not by a Williams, but by Mr J.S. Corbett, agent for the Bute estate. It is now known as the Cedar Tree (formerly Corbetts Hotel).

Pwll-y-pant House, 1930s.

Mr Frank Thomas penning sheep at Ysgubor Wen Farm, Groeswen, 1921.

Group of Groeswen gentlemen, 1921. From left to right, back row: Garfield, Morgan and Willie Roberts. Front row: -?-, Frank Thomas.

Frank Thomas of Ysgubor Wen Farm pictured with his prize-winning sheepdog, 1920s.

Bryn Owen Farm, between Caerphilly and Llanbradach, *c.* 1951. Typical of the local upland farms, many of which have disappeared from the area since the Second World War, it was demolished by the Forestry Commission in the 1950s.

Llanbradach Fawr, 1930s. This was for many generations the home of the Thomas family, the prominent Glamorgan land-owning family. It is probably the oldest occupied dwelling in the area, dating from the sixteenth century. It was the demesne farm of the Llanbradach Estate which consisted of five farms including Bryn Owen (above) and Graddfa (opposite). Of these, Tynygraig Farm was entirely swallowed up by the pit village of Llanbradach during the 1890s.

Graddfa, Llanbradach, 1955. The original farm on this site was the birthplace in 1760 of the Rev. Morgan John Rhys, preacher, publisher, promoter of the Welsh language and founder of a Welsh colony at Cambria, Pennsylvania.

Tonyfelin House, 1968. This was the former home of Henry Anthony, the mill-owner at Tonyfelin.

The "tithe barn" belonging to Castle Farm, Caerphilly, 1954. It stood on the side of Crescent Road near the junction with Nantgarw Road until its demolition in the early 1960s.

Dadleudy or Court House, 1951. This was built in the fourteenth century and was thus named since royal and manorial courts were once held here. It replaced an earlier court, which was held in the south gatehouse of the castle, and was constructed on part of the burgage (house plot) of a Thomas le Warde. Later, Dadleudy became the home of the Price family, a branch of which also lived at Pontypandy House and Watford Fawr. Today the building is a public house.

Three

Industry and Trade

Energlyn corn mill shortly before its closure, c. 1910. It stood opposite the old gasworks site in Mill Road, near the council bus depot. Morgan Street in Caerphilly was named after the family of Frederick Morgan, pictured above, who was the miller at the time this postcard was first made. Note that the image has been manipulated with cascading water scratched onto the negative to heighten the dramatic appeal and thereby increase sales of the card. In reality, only one of the wheels was running. The retouching of postcard negatives was common practice at this time; instead of reshooting a scene a photographer might "freshen up" a negative by adding a new motor car or erasing a vanished building.

The old Castle Woollen Mill in 1936 shortly before its demolition as part of the renovation and rebuilding of Caerphilly Castle and its surrounds. Note the castle walls and the Clive Arms on Cardiff Road, top left. The 1871 Census lists 36 workers as employed in the woollen industry in the Caerphilly area amounting to approximately 6 per cent of the working population. This figure, however, greatly underestimates the total activity, because of the many people who wove or made their own cloth domestically. The Castle mill was closed at the end of the nineteenth century and ended its days as Pym's Tearooms.

Surface workers at the Rhos Llantwit Colliery, c. 1885. This was sited near Bedwas Road where part of the Lansbury Park housing development now stands. It produced coal from 1864 to 1892 and supplied the first Caerphilly gas works which was situated "next door". The streets of Caerphilly were first illuminated by gas light in December 1968.

Rhos Llantwit Colliery, c. 1885. Prior to the opening of the Glamorganshire Canal at the end of the eighteenth century, coal had been supplied to Cardiff from a number of small levels in the Caerphilly district. Through the first half of the nineteenth century, while other areas in South Wales were transformed by the industrial revolution, Caerphilly, remained a small village providing a market for its rural hinterland. However, as in other similar places, the coming of the railway saw any sleepiness wiped rapidly away. In 1859 a branch of the Rhymney Railway was opened to Caerphilly thereby providing a convenient means of exporting coal from the area. Mines sprang up like mushrooms in this period, for example at Energlyn, Wernddu and other sites. 1863 saw the sinking by the Machen Colliery Company of the pictured pit on the land of Porset Farm and in the following August the first coal was sent to Newport. In 1866 the lease was transferred to the Rhos Llantwit Company who renamed the pit. In 1871 a new shaft was sunk and although the concern suffered from the fluctuations in demand for its coal, by 1880 it was a flourishing concern regularly producing 70,000 tons a year. Increasingly difficult mining conditions, as the coal seams became worked out, brought the colliery's life to a sudden end, however, and the lease was abandoned when it came up for renewal in 1892. Rhos Llantwit was closed, as was the Energlyn site which had been maintained as a pumping station. The growth of the mining industry transformed the socio-economic profile of the area: from an 1861 population of 1,047 by 1881 Caerphilly had swelled to a town of over 3,000 inhabitants as colliers and their families moved into the area, many of them from the West of England. In 1891 the Caerphilly, Bedwas, Machen and Rudry Miners' Association had almost 1,200 members. While collieries in the immediate vicinity of Caerphilly were short-lived the sinking of a succession of pits nearby meant that mining remained the dominant occupation in Caerphilly until well into the twentieth century, shaping the character of the town through work and unemployment. The sinking of large collieries began at Llanbradach (1887), Senghenydd (1893), Abertridwr (1898), Bedwas (1913) and Nantgarw (1915). All employed a large number of Caerphilly men.

Llanbradach Colliery, *c.* 1900. No. 1 shaft, sunk to a depth of 1,716 feet, was completed here in November 1890 while the 1,752 feet No. 2 shaft was finished by April 1894. In 1914 the colliery employed 2,500 men and boys. Eighty-eight workers were killed in the first 25 years of the colliery's history including eight men in an explosion in 1901.

Officials at Llanbradach Colliery during the lockout of the miners in 1921.

"King Freddie" of Buganda – a former kingdom in East Africa absorbed by Uganda after 1963 – pictured during his visit to Llanbradach Colliery, 1950s. He is accompanied by Cornelius Hughes the pit manager.

A chimney stack being demolished, Llanbradach Colliery, 27 February 1965. The colliery had officially stopped production on 29 December 1961.

Universal Colliery, Senghenydd, *c.* 1912. The history of mining in the Caerphilly area is blighted by what happened here at Senghenydd in 1913. On the morning of Tuesday 14 October 439 men and boys were killed at the western (Lancaster) workings of the Universal Colliery in Britain's worst mining disaster. One of the rescue team also died. An explosion of methane, in what was a notoriously fiery pit – the lives of 81 men had already been claimed here on 24 May 1901 – ignited coal dust triggering a massive second explosion which ripped through the tunnels and shafts. The colliery closed its relatively short and tragic life in 1928 falling victim to the depression. The long shadow cast by the disaster still lingers, however. The last of the Senghenydd widows died in 1994 and many of the children of the victims are still alive to remember and mourn.

Windsor Colliery, Abertridwr, *c.* 1912.

Llanbradach Industrial Co-operative Society, *c*. 1914. It had branches at Caerphilly, Bedwas and Ystrad Mynach

Delivering milk in Tynygraig Road, Llanbradach, *c*. 1950.

Mr T.F. Howells, master builder and entrepreneur in the Caerphilly area. He built various private and public buildings in the town including the Castle Cinema (1912) and the Blue Bell for Josiah Morgan, with whom he started the Mynyddislwyn Colliery Company; and the National Provincial Bank (now Nat West) in Cardiff Road. He died in 1929 at the age of fifty-nine.

Caerphilly Fellmongers Ltd (formerly the site of the Tonyfelin Woollen Mill), 1956. The building was known locally as the tanyard although it was actually used for the preparation of hides and sheepskins, prior to tanning. The area was nicknamed "Lavender Corner" for obvious reasons.

Harris Corn Stores, Twyn, Caerphilly, 1951. This building was demolished in 1968.

Market Hall on the Twyn, 1951 shortly before its demolition. Opened in 1889, it was the site of the Caerphilly cheese market until 1910.

Advertisement for Manchester House and E. & E. Davies, drapers of Cardiff Road, which appeared in the Borough Guide to Caerphilly, c. 1911.

Manchester House, drapers, Twyn, pictured shortly before the business closed in 1980.

Four

Transport

The branch line to Senghenydd which opened on 1 February 1894 to service the new colliery, the sinking of which has started the previous year. The development of all corners of the South Wales coalfield through the second half of the nineteenth century saw the creation of a fantastic web of train networks. Rival rail and colliery companies battled for dominance over the transportation of coal and coal products to the markets of Britain and the world.

This 1920s view of the coke ovens at Llanbradach portrays emphatically the symbiotic relationship between the railway and the mines and gives an indication of the extent of colliery-related freight that was transported daily through the South Wales valleys.

Passenger train entering Llanbradach station, probably on an excursion to Barry from the Pontypool area.

Management and employees at the Caerphilly Locomotive, Carriage and Wagon Works (popularly known as the "Sheds"), 1930s. They were opened in 1901 by the Rhymney Railway becoming a major employer in the town. Between 1922 and 1947 the works were operated by the Great Western Railway, which expanded them in 1926 and 1939. Following the "dieselisation" of the railway system the "Sheds" were closed in January 1964.

Caerphilly Castle, the first engine out of the Swindon Works after the First World War and pioneer of a class of steam locomotives built by the Great Western Railway Company for twenty years. It had covered 1,910,630 miles by the time of its withdrawal from service on 10 May 1960. It is now on display at the Science Museum in London.

The dismantling of the 2,400 foot long Llanbradach Viaduct, 1937. This impressive, but short-lived structure was completed in 1904 at a cost of £250,000. It carried the Barry Railway (1884–1921), after it had skirted Caerphilly town, 125 feet above the valley floor to the east side of the Rhymney river where it joined up with the Brecon and Merthyr line. The owners of the Barry docks thus hoped to attract freight in the area away from Cardiff and Newport.

One of the girders which fell over the river, 1937. The spectacular demolition of the viaduct attracted much attention; many local schools took their pupils along to witness the event and a commentary was broadcast on the wireless.

Workmen involved in the dismantling of Llanbradach Viaduct, 1937–38.

Coal which, as the cheapest available filling material at the time of construction, had been used to pack the pillars of the viaduct is shown here being collected during the dismantling process.

Aerial view of Caerphilly looking west, c. 1955, showing "The Sheds" in the foreground to the right of the railway line. Note how small the town is, seen here before the major housing developments of recent decades. The line leading off to the right is the branch of the Brecon and Merthyr Railway constructed in 1861, while beyond the station the track splits with the left line going to Pontypridd and the right line continuing up the valley to Rhymney. The picture shows how the railway formed in some ways a social barrier between the houses of the middle class up the hillside to the left and those of the working class on the right.

A new car, reputedly the first to be owned in Llanbradach, pictured here at the rear of the Llanbradach Hotel, 1904. It belonged to the licensee, Mr Fussell. (photograph lent by Miss Elsie Davies)

Caerphilly railway station, Cardiff Road, 1977. Caerphilly has long been within the Cardiff commuter belt and, before the advent of widespread car ownership, the railway provided an essential daily link for the middle management in the city.

Caerphilly bus station, 1957. It was replaced by the new bus terminus in the summer of 1973.

Caerphilly bus station, 1962.

Five
Caerphilly: Cardiff Road and the Twyn

Cardiff Road, *c*. 1897. Until the middle of the nineteenth century the town of Caerphilly consisted of the Piccadilly Square, Castle Street and the Twyn. It was not until the 1860s that the construction began of houses along what is now Cardiff Road. The white building on the right was the stables of the King's Arms public house next door. It contained a malthouse on the upper floor.

Cardiff Road, 1920s.

Cardiff Road, *c.* 1939. The delivery cart belonged to Ernest Coleman, baker and confectioner. Percy, his brother and business partner, was an auctioneer and also Chief Officer of the local fire service.

Cardiff Road, 1964.

Cardiff Road, 1968. The building at the bend in the road with the two gable windows was the first known Wesleyan Methodist church in Caerphilly. Following the departure of the congregation in 1868 to a new church in Castle Street, the Primitive Methodists worshipped here until in 1888 they too moved into their new church on Pontygwindy Road (see p.77).

Lower end of Cardiff Road, showing the newly built Clive Hotel which replaced the old inn, 1890s.

Lower end of Cardiff Road, *c.* 1912. On the left next to the bank is the lane leading to the footpath alongside the castle to Nantgarw Road. On the other side of the lane are the Wedlock Cottages and Harrison & Hann, solicitors. In the distance facing the camera is the Twyn Chapel with its clock tower and the side of Tŷ Vaughan, then the premises of the London & Provincial Bank, later Barclays (see p.54).

Lower end of Cardiff Road, *c*. 1968. The demolition of the Clive Arms on the right began in December 1970.

View of Cardiff Road from the Twyn, *c*. 1910.

Tŷ Vaughan, Twyn, 1930s. The building was named after William Vaughan, a trader here at the end of the eighteenth and beginning of the nineteenth century

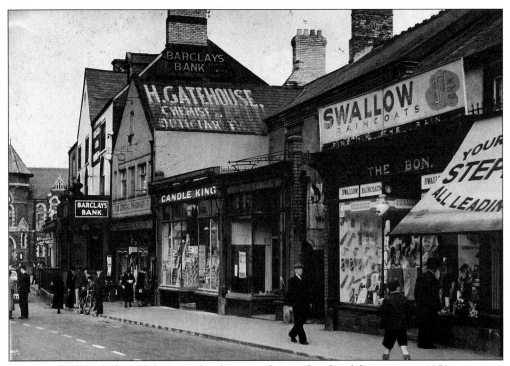

Lower end of Cardiff Road showing the shops on the south side of the street, *c*. 1950.

Doctor's Hill Caerphilly, *c.* 1934, showing a Western Welsh bus exiting Cardiff Road. Tŷ Vaughan, Gatehouse, chemist and Candle King (which specialised in the sale of cheap vegetable and dried salt fish) are visible top left. To the right of the bus on the corner is Wookey's House and, next to it, Castle House. The Clive Arms Hotel on Cardiff Road can also be seen, top right. The buildings on the north side of Cardiff Road were demolished in the 1930s and some of the stone, perhaps originally quarried from the castle itself, was loaded into trams and transported along a light gauge track back to the castle. There it was used as a building material during reconstruction.

The Twyn, *c.* 1938. The steeples of the Van Road Church (left) and the Twyn Chapel, the Welsh Calvinistic Methodist Church (right centre) can be seen immediately behind the premises of Harris, corn stores and Owen Jones, printer, respectively. Visible on the far left are the ruins of the corn market, facing the Blue Bell Inn, and on the far right, the new post office.

The Twyn, *c.* 1936. From left to right the premises were: Pontypridd Furnishers, Boar's Head Inn, Castle Cinema, Owen Jones, printer.

View of Tŷ Vaughan from outside the post office, 1967, showing the Twyn Laundry.

Bute Close, Twyn, Caerphilly, 1967. The site is now occupied by a car park. In the background the rear of Windsor Street can be seen.

View of the Twyn from Caerphilly Castle, 1972.

Boarded-up premises of the Twyn Chinese Laundry once run by Mr Ng, as viewed from the former Twyn Chapel, *c.* 1968.

Six

Caerphilly:
Castle Street
to Piccadilly Square

Castle Street, *c.* 1900.

Castle Street looking towards the Twyn, *c.* 1900.

Castle Street and the foot of the Twyn, *c.* 1914. To the left is Market Street with the Crown Inn, the Boars Head Inn, the Castle Cinema and the newly built Blue Bell Inn which replaced a much older public house of the same name. In the centre is an open space sometimes called the Crown Square or simply "the Square". Behind are the Underhill Chambers burnt down in the disastrous fire of 1922 which led to the formation of Caerphilly Fire Brigade. At the back of this building is the short stretch of Mansel Street with the labour exchange on the corner. To the right the back of Dr Llewellyn's house can be seen and beyond it Tŷ Vaughan on the Twyn. In between these two buildings a roundabout is visible. This would have belonged to the fair which was held on the Twyn in August. After the First World War the pleasure fair was held at the back of the Workmen's Hall, an area which became known as the Fair Field.

Piccadilly Square, Caerphilly, *c.* 1900.

Piccadilly Square, Caerphilly, *c.* 1930. Josiah Morgan, well-known local entrepreneur and one-time licensee at the Piccadilly Inn, regularly paid for the sweeping of the square on Sunday mornings so that it would appear clean and tidy on this day of worship.

End of the Old Bailey, near Piccadilly Square, 1930s. This was demolished about 1936. In a cottage behind the Bailey, Evan James, who wrote the words of the Welsh National Anthem, was born on 4 October 1809, as recorded in the Eglwysilan parish register.

The west side of Castle Street, 1933.

View along Castle Street towards Piccadilly Square, *c.* 1936. On the left were Lorimore, saddler; the White Lion Inn and Evan Rees, butcher and bookmaker. The light strip indicates the position of a passage to the smithy behind the White Lion Inn while visible in the distance, behind the approaching car, is the Old Bailey. On the right of the street is the distinctive facade of the Old Armoury; Ruther Jones, greengrocer and with the three brass balls clearly indicating his shop, Shibko the pawnbroker.

Castle Street, 1936. From left to right the buildings were: Corbett, second-hand dealer; the Queen's Hotel (in the process of demolition); the Emporium; Lorimore, saddler.

Castle Street as pictured from the castle walls, 1969.

Castle Hotel, *c.* 1968.

Star Supply Stores, Castle Street.

The "Old Armoury" at the junction of Castle Street and Bedwas Road, c. 1970. This building was constructed on the site of a cottage that was used as an armoury by the Caerphilly Volunteers during the Napoleonic Wars. In 1919 the Prudential Assurance Company opened its new Caerphilly offices here.

Castle Street in the mid-1950s.

View from Piccadilly Square up Castle Street, 1968.

Castle Street, 1968.

Castle Street, 1968.

The Castle Street end of Bedwas Road, 1969. The cottages were demolished in the early 1970s.

Tonyfelin Road, Caerphilly, 1969 looking towards the tanyard. The houses were demolished in the early 1970s.

Seven
Religion

St Martin's Church, Caerphilly.

St Martin's Church, Caerphilly, c. 1900, showing the building before the 1905 extension and the addition of the tower in 1910–11. There has been a place of worship on this site since at least the sixteenth century and would originally have been a chapel-of-ease for the parish of Eglwysilan. In 1867, however, St Martin's was separated from Eglwysilan becoming the parish church of Caerphilly and in 1879 a new church, pictured above, was built. The older building was removed a few years later. The first chapel was probably built here shortly after the construction of the castle and served the newly planted town first occupied primarily by non-native (i.e. English) inhabitants.

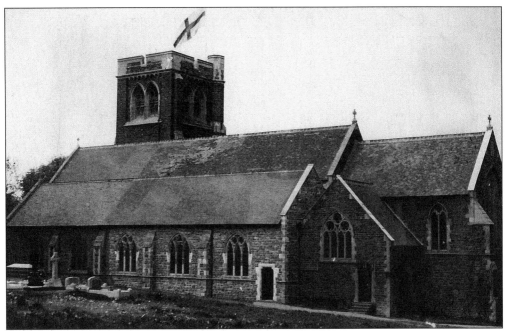

St Martin's Church pictured after the south aisle was completed in 1938. It was dedicated in May of that year by the Bishop of Llandaff, the Rt. Rev. Timothy Rees. Much of the £2,000 cost of the work was met by fundraising activities such as fetes.

Concert held in St Martin's Church, 1960s.

St Martin's Church,
Caerphilly in May 1951 after
the trees near the tower had
been chopped down.

Mothers Union, outside St Catherine's Church, Mill Road, Caerphilly, 1923.

St Catherine's Church choir, 1923.

Wesleyan Methodist Chapel on Castle Street. It was opened on 24 July 1868 as the first English language non-conformist cause in the town. Following its closure and rapid demolition in the late 1920s as part of the remodelling of the area around the castle, a new Wesleyan chapel was opened in Crescent Road.

English Congregational Church, Van Road, Caerphilly. The cause was established in 1898 and the foundation stones for a new church were laid on 23 November 1903. It helped to satisfy the religious needs of the increasing numbers of monoglot English speakers in the area.

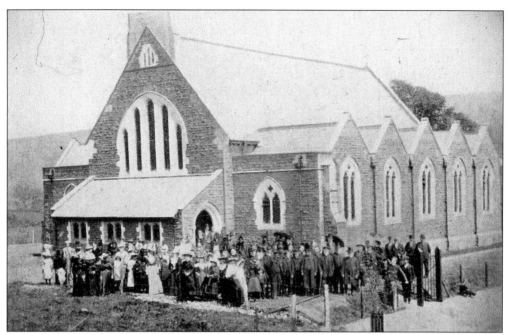

The dedication of All Saints church, Llanbradach, by the Bishop of Llandaff in 1897. The chancel, vestries and a 66 ft high tower were added in 1909 and a peal of eight bells was installed in 1911. The building was declared unsafe and stood unused for several ywears before being demolished in 1994.

Boxing club, All Saints church, Llanbradach, *c.* 1910. The boy, front centre, is holding weighted clubs which were used in forearm strengthening excercises by the lads. The Revd Edwin Edwards served the parish as curate and vicar for 25 yeras until his death in 1928.

Ebenezer Church, Llanbradach, *c.* 1910.

Minister and deacons at the Seion Chapel, Llanbradach, 1931 when the Rev. Esaias Hopkins began his ministry there. From left to right, back row: Moses Butler, Ellis Hughes, Robert Hopkins, Hugh Griffiths, John Evans. Front row: John Williams, Richard Jarman, Esaias Hopkins, Edward Morgan, Thomas Nicholas.

Groeswen Chapel near Caerphilly, 1960s. The first building here was opened in 1742; this was enlarged in 1766 and in 1879. One of the early ministers was William Edwards who was to win considerable fame as the architect of the single arch bridge at Pontypridd.

The sisterhood at Salem Chapel, Senghenydd, 1948.

The Primitive Methodist Chapel, Pontygwyndy Road, opened 1888 (left) and the Bethel Congregational Chapel on Nantgarw Road (right), *c.* 1972. The first Bethel chapel in the town was situated in Castle Street before the opening of the new building on Nantgarw Road on Easter Sunday 1895.

Watford Chapel, *c.* 1956. It was originally opened in 1739 by the Rev. David Williams of Pwll-y-pant, a leading evangeliser in the area.

Old Tonyfelin Baptist Chapel (used from 1784), Caerphilly with the minister's house on the left, 1956.

Tonyfelin Chapel, 1965. This opened in 1866 to accommodate some eight hundred people and replaced the first chapel pictured above. Shortly after this photograph was taken, the wall was removed and 129 graves were excavated, with the remains of the dead being reinterred at Penyrheol Cemetery. The work enabled Caerphilly Urban District Council to widen the road at this busy junction and provide a pavement.

Eight
Children and Education

Coed-y-Brain Infants School, Llanbradach, *c.* 1909. This school was opened on 29 August 1900 by Eglwysilan School Board.

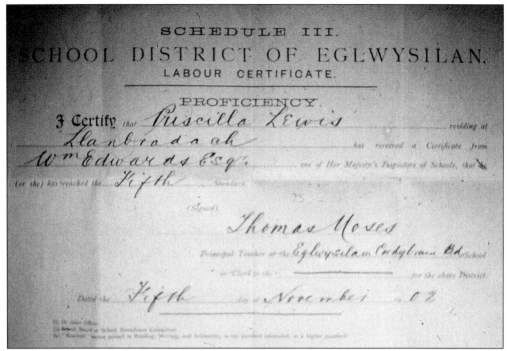

Labour certificate from 1902 confirming that the pupil could leave school to start work. (lent by Miss Elsie Davies)

Pupils of Hendre School holding a St David's Day tea party in Energlyn Terrace, *c.* 1921.

Pupils of Hendre School, *c.* 1925.

Caerphilly Girls Secondary School, *c.* 1929. The two teachers are Miss Pearce (left) and Miss Grant (later headmistress).

The Farmer children, *c.* 1921. From left to right: Hattie Wavery Farmer, Ivy May Farmer, Robert Arthur Farmer.

Girls of the Twyn Council School at Caerphilly railway station, *c.* 1930, ready to embark on a trip to London with the scholarship teacher at the school, Miss Dora Brown (standing at the back below the lamp). She was later head of Gwyndy Senior School and Gwyndy Secondary Modern School.

Mill Road Infants School, Caerphilly, *c.* 1934. Seated on the far left of the picture is Glyndwr G. Jones, later author of *Cronicl Caerffili*, the comprehensive history of the town published between 1973 and 1985.

Scholarship class at Gwyndy School, Pontygwyndy Road, Caerphilly, *c.* 1937. Entrance to the Caerphilly boys and girls secondary schools was at this time by means of competitive examination. The small percentage of children considered sufficiently able to try for a place were tutored in scholarship classes in the junior schools. From left to right, back row: John

A view from Pontygwyndy Road of the Gwyndy Senior Girls School which was opened in September 1933.

Powell, Glyndwr G. Jones, Gordon Powell, Lionel Williams, Gwyn Parry, Aneurin Davies, Royston Davies, Ken Newman, Ivor Shattock, Howard Tarrant. Front row: Mary Adams, Dorothy Davies, Joyce Abbot, Beryl Mortimer, Edith Cavell, Jean Williams, Naroma Brooks, Lilian Bayliss, Dorothy Whitefoot, Eileen Phillips, Beryl Morgan, Alda Davy.

Teachers at Gwyndy Senior Girls School with Miss Dora Brown (headmistress) seated centre, October 1948. On her right is Ruth Allen, an exchange scheme teacher from Michigan, USA.

Class 3A P.T. group with Mrs Eluned Thomas, Gwyndy Senior Girls School, October 1948.

Second year boys at Caerphilly Boys' Secondary School, 1945–46 school year. The "Butler" Education Act of 1944 designated the school as a Secondary Grammar, an official status which was adopted in 1947. In 1953 it was amalgamated with Caerphilly Technical School under the new title of Caerphilly Grammar Technical School. This school, in turn, became St Martin's Comprehensive School in September 1973.

Fifth Form at Caerphilly Girls' Grammar School, 1946. From left to right, back row: Mary McBride, Heather Williams, Glenna Moses, Jean Walters, Olga Roberts. Middle row: Jean Tudor, Shirley ?, Jean Thomas, Katherine Davies, Gwen Hughes, June Leader. Front row: Mona Rowlands, -?-, Pat Carragher, Miss Adams (teacher), Jean Williams, Beryl Lewis, Joan Roberts.

Standard II at Coed-y-Brain Junior School, Llanbradach, 1946. From left to right, back row: Mrs Davies (teacher), Keith Butler, Duggie Powell, John Srodzinski, Glyn Jones, Vernon Spragg, Frankie Pascoe, Eddie Jones, ? Parry, Charlie Rowlands, Tom Howell Jones (headmaster). Middle row: Peter Davies, Billy Gater, Jimmy Hudd, Ivor Pugh, Brian Kearle, Arthur Osbourne, John Payne, Peter Lane, David Metters, Jimmy Pym, Billy Lowell. Front row: Billy Tilley, Christopher Dee, Teddie Kenyon, -?-, David Osbourne, Tommy Edwards, Idris Brimble, Bobby Jones, Jimmy Poole, Dennis Brown.

Top class at Gwyndy Infants' School, Caerphilly, 1948. From left to right, top row: Desmond Pask, Terry Wheeler, -?-, Ann Lewis, Margaret Brimble, Bronwen Difford, Briony Moore, Tony Cecil, Gwyn Ferris. Third row: Marjorie Jayne, Joan Bevan, Gillian Davies, Barbara Thomas, Valerie Lewis, Marjorie Gadd, Margaret White, Ann Nicholas, Ann Bevan. Second Row: Kay Geen, Janice Roberts, Geraldine Mayo, Julie Thorn, Joan Davies, Marilyn Davies, June Hayward, Pamela Thatcher. Front row: Alan Richards, Geoffrey ? , Tony Packham, Lyn Jones, Peter Griffiths, Norman ? .

Senghenydd Junior School, 1950.

Children from Gwyndy and Twyn Schools at a joint concert, early 1950s.

Abertridwr *Adran yr Urdd*, pictured on the steps of Caerphilly Boys' Grammar School in 1957. From left to right, back row: Hywel Evans, Geraint Evans, Brenda Evans, Paul Anzani. Fourth row: Annwyn Griffiths, Jane Morgan, Elizabeth Jones, Meriel Roberts, Gillian Snelling. Third row: Pearl Silcox, Ann Taylor, Pat Waddon, Marjorie Bright, Meryl Hunt. Second row: Amy Evans, Enydd Lewis, Jennet Morgan, ? Bevan, Vilma Laybourne. Front row: -?-, ? Bevan, Edward Lloyd, Eric Silcox, Heddwyn Davies.

Pupils at Caerphilly Grammar Technical School, 1968.

The old Tonyfelin Board School, 1977. This building, which in its latter years was used by the engineers department of Rhymney Valley District Council, was demolished in 1984.

Nine
Serving the Community

Morgan Roberts, Groeswen, one of the many local men who served their country in the First World War.

Caerphilly section of the Special Constabulary, Glamorgan Police, 1940. Officers, commencing second on the left, front row: S. Sgt. C. Newman, S. Sgt. H. Knight, J. Lassman (with medals), S. Inspector H. Gatehouse, Regular Inspector A. Morris, Regular Superintendent Howell Rees, F. Div. S. Chief Inspector J.A. Nicholas, S. Inspector W. Taylor, S. Sgt. E. Watts, S. Sgt. W. Lewis, S. Sgt. M.W. Rees. With his distinctive waxed moustache, Joe Lassman was a well-known Caerphilly character. An old soldier, he sported more medals from half forgotten campaigns than any other person in the town. He served in the Home Guard, the Army Cadets and the Air Training Corps (where he was bandmaster) sporting a separate uniform for each role. He also played the Last Post on his bugle every Armistice Day.

Llanbradach Home Guard during the Second World War.

US servicemen, probably stationed at Barry, pose during their tour of Caerphilly Castle under the guidance of the custodian, Mr William (Bill) Bassett, *c.* 1944.

Ben Schneider, the American G.I. who was billeted for a short while with the Gatehouse family in Caerphilly. From left to right, H.J. Gatehouse, Ben Schneider, Peter Gatehouse, Mrs H.J. Gatehouse. There was an American army camp off Pontygwyndy Road in buildings originally constructed by Glamorgan County Council as an alternative headquarters, in case they were forced to leave Cardiff as a result of German bombing. The 756 Railway Shop Battalion arrived in 1943 and left Caerphilly on 17 May 1944 during the build-up to the D Day invasion of France. The arrival of American G.I.s in the area caused quite a stir and no little envy amongst some. Well-paid at £15 per month compared to the average of £4 for the British private soldier, the strict petrol rationing seemed not to apply as they drove around the area in their jeeps. This relative "glamour" in the austere wartime climate attracted local girls for whom a bus service was operated enabling them to attend dances at the camp. However, the Yanks were generally remembered as generous and polite visitors – the pestering chant of "got any gum, chum?" from local children, for example, rarely went unrewarded.

Dedication of the tablet added to the cenotaph in Caerphilly, bearing the names of those killed in service during the Second World War and also those of two civilians killed during their work at the ordnance factory in Llanishen.

Lieutenant Commander R.E.S. Hugonin and Sub-lieut. A.W. Goodworth pose with the Welsh crew members of HMS Woodpecker in 1943. Among those pictured are A.H. Srodzinski of Llanbradach and C.S. Jones of Bedwas. The Woodpecker was successful as part of the Second Escort Group protecting Allied convoys in the Atlantic and Arctic Oceans from attack by German U-boats. She was sunk by a German torpedo in February 1944. Service during the Second World War, brought together men in a melting pot experience and forged links of friendship many of which have lasted a lifetime, as the recent fiftieth anniversary celebrations have shown.

Llanbradach "Toc H" branch, pictured outside All Saints' Church, c. 1950. From left to right, back row: Walter Wright, Trevor Thomas, Jack Rees, Harry Bowsher, Myrddin Dole, Owen Quartley, Iorwerth Jones, Jack Hardacre, Stan Stenick, Bill Martin, Dennis Sellwood. Front row: Southey Parrish, Bert Sellwood, Dai Thornton, Vic Hardacre (the well-known local photographer), W.H. Wells, Percy Colson, Tom Phillips. "Toc H" was a male fellowship and social club with branches throughout the country; it was originally formed in France during the First World War. At Llanbradach the members held their meetings in the old co-op bakery.

Caerphilly District Miners' Hospital. At a meeting in 1919 it was agreed to purchase the house called the Beeches, near Watford, Caerphilly, from its owner, Mr Frederick Pigott and to convert this into a hospital. A mass assembly of miners was held in the Palace Theatre, Caerphilly in July 1920 at which the men decided that they would pay 6d each per week to meet the cost of the conversion. The completed hospital was opened on 30 June 1923 by County Councillor John Phillips of Nelson, Chairman of the Hospital Committee and the first patients were admitted two days later. In total some ten thousand miners contributed from their wages raising approximately £36,000 in what was a formidable display of community solidarity.

Brothers F.W. and H.J. Gatehouse, whose contribution to the photographic history of Caerphilly is well worthy of mention. H.J. Gatehouse's son, Peter, who currently runs the chemist's shop started by his father on Cardiff Road, is the only Caerphilly born player to have represented Glamorgan Cricket Club. Between 1957 and 1962 he made 23 first class appearances for the county taking 53 wickets at an average of just over 29.

Ness Edwards MP (1939–1968 and Postmaster-General in the second Attlee government 1950–51), in the striped suit, unveils the memorial to Morgan Jones (Member of Parliament for the area from 1921 until his death in 1939 and the first conscientious objector to sit in the House of Commons), Caerphilly, 1953. Previously part of the Glamorgan East seat, Caerphilly became a parliamentary division as a result of the Representation of the People Act of June 1918, covering an area as far north as Pontlottyn and including Deri and Fochriw within its boundary. Under this act all men over the age of twenty-one and all women over the age of thirty were eligible to vote. This consolidation of mass democracy – there were now 32,790 voters – provided the opportunity for the Labour Party to establish a stronghold which has lasted through the rest of this century. In the general election of 1918 Alfred Onions, formerly Treasurer of the South Wales Miners' Federation, won the seat with 54.8% of the vote and was carried through the streets by his jubilant Labour supporters.

Llanbradach Chamber of Trade supplying Christmas cheer to the children of Coed-y-brain School, c. 1957. Among those pictured are Trevor Parry, Irvine Piper, Aubrey Jenkins, Vic Stone, Iris Stone, Tom Jones (headmaster at the school), Llew Thomas and Arthur Smith. Father Christmas was played by Charles Snook.

Ten

Events

A decorated Castle Street in preparation for the visit of King Edward VII and Queen Alexandra to the town, 13 July 1907. The streets of the town were lined with thousands of local people cheering the Royal Couple.

The Piccadilly Inn being decorated for the royal visit of 1907.

Cardiff Road decorated for the royal visit of 1907. It is interesting to compare this view with that of the later one on p. 51.

King George V and Queen Mary at Caerphilly Castle, 26 June 1912 during their tour of South Wales.

The royal visit, Caerphilly Castle, 1912. Arrangements for this visit were marred by a disagreement between the head teachers and assistant teachers in the district over the appointment of a conductor for the welcoming childrens' choir, with the result that a programme of music to be performed by 1,200 children was abandoned.

VE Day celebrations at Caerphilly Golf Club, 1945.

VE Day celebrations in Senghenydd, June 1945. From left to right, back row: Gwladys Roberts, Mrs Williams, Mrs Davies, Rosie John, Vera Kestell, Mrs Morgan, Betty Jones, Margaret Hughes, Marion Williams, Katie Pugh. Front row: Audrey Shelding, Mrs Owen, Iris Lewis, Mrs Lewis, Miss Williams, Mrs Isaac, Mrs Davies.

Gorsedd ceremony at the National Eisteddfod of Wales held at Caerffili in 1950, showing Cynan (Rev. W.E. Jones) on the logan stone receiving the Horn of Plenty from Mam y Fro. Trefin (Mr Edgar Phillips) the Archdruid holds the Eisteddod sword on the left of the logan stone. Crwys (Rev. Crwys Williams), a former archdruid, is pictured far right.

Crwys, Trefin and another bard holding the Eisteddfod sword. The Gorsedd ceremony was performed in Parc Dafydd Williams bordering Caerphilly Castle, with the Eisteddfod itself being held in the grounds of the girls' grammar school (now St Ilan Comprehensive School).

Caerphilly Mixed Grammar Schools orchestra which took part in the National Eisteddfod, 1950. The group includes: Telfryn Thomas, Donald Kitt, Michael Pugh, Mr Roger Jones, Vivian Jones, Beverley ?, Edward Griffiths, Berwick Williams, Brian Samuels, David Williams, ? Richards, Eleri Richards.

Pentrebane Street, Caerphilly, photographed in August 1950 during the National Eisteddfod week. The entrance to the Plymouth Hall can be seen on the right.

Junior dance team from Gwyndy Senior Girls School which won a second prize at the Caerphilly National Eisteddfod in 1950. The teacher was Mrs Eluned Thomas.

Team from Gwyndy Senior Girls School which won a first prize for dancing in the junior section at the National Eisteddfod.

Archdruid Cynan conducts the crowning ceremony at the Caerphilly National Eisteddfod in 1950. The victorious bard is the Rev. Euros Bowen.

These three pictures show the street party held in Heol Aneurin as part of the celebrations of the Investiture of Prince Charles as Prince of Wales, 1969.

Eleven

Clubs, Leisure
and Entertainment

A Primrose League outing pictured "before the off" outside the Railway Hotel in Caerphilly, 1920s.

Llanbradach Park, c. 1930. Officially opened in May 1930, this was one of the finest parks in the area. When the job of gardener/groundsman was advertised in the national press, some 200 applications were received from all over the country.

Llanbradach Glee Party, 1940. Among those pictured are: Lloydie Jones, Myra Jarman, Priscilla Williams, Eira Rist, Blodwen Shannon, Mary Parsons, Cassie Williams, Dick Rist, Gwladys Hughes, Catherine Rist, Louisa Watkins, Lissie Shannon, Sylvia James.

Jazz band outside the Castle Cinema, Caerphilly, 1947.

Llanbradach hop-pickers departing for a "working holiday" in Herefordshire, *c.* 1950.

Caerphilly Boys Secondary Grammar School's summer camp, 1948, at Oxwich on the Gower.

Representatives from Caerphilly to the Dolgellau National Eisteddfod, 1949. From left to right: Iorwerth Thomas, Jordan Davies, Cllr Snell, T.W. Thomas (Pentyrch), Herbert P. Richards, Rev. Josiah Knight, Miss Mary Thomas, Maldwyn Howells (behind Miss Thomas), Glyn Lloyd (Secretary of Caerphilly Eisteddfod), Lloyd Jones (Caerphilly UDC), D.J. Owen (headmaster at Hengoed), Dr Iorwerth C. Peate (St Fagans), Rev. Rhys Bowen (Rhymney), John Beynon, Mr Thomas (Bedwas), D.W. Davies, Mr Williams (National Provincial Bank).

Senghenydd old age pensioners showing off their Easter bonnets, 1955.

Senghenydd old age pensioners.

St Cenydd Choir, 1948. Among those pictured are Natalie Jenkins, Joan Price, Gaynor Morgan, Beryl Hyatt, Jane Derrick, Beryl Hughes, Joyce Morgan, Iris Hughes, Marie Roach, Dwynwen Evans, Pam Jenkins, Megan Wilson, Christine Howells, Agnes Higgins, Joan Roberts, Rowena Howells, Joyce Bowden, Peggy Cartwright, Gill Isaac, Brenda Woods, Brenda Roberts, Beryl Jones, Eirwen Jones, Judith Jenkins, Ann McDougal, Gill Roberts, Elizabeth Jones.

The Margaret Roach Singers giving a performance of "old time" music hall, Rudry Village Hall, December 1968. The choir was formed in January 1966 by Mrs Margaret Roach and a core of ex-members of the disbanded St Cenydd Ladies Choir. Mrs Roach retired from conducting the choir in 1973 and was replaced as Musical Director by Mrs Margaret Webb. Mrs Jean Davies has been accompanist for the choir for the majority of its history, from 1966 to 1971 and from 1976 to date. Over the years the choir has raised several thousands of pounds for various charities and its members have acted as musical ambassadors for both Caerphilly and the Rhymney Valley.

The Margaret Roach Singers pictured during a performance at the "49" Club, Caerphilly, March 1970.

Caerphilly Male Voice Choir pictured outside Caerphilly Castle, April 1919. The President was W.A. Phillips J.P. and the conductor was Mr Jordan Davies.

Caerphilly Male Voice Choir, pictured upstairs at the Blue Bell, 1956. The choir was originally formed in 1906 by a group of Caerphilly cricketers who wished to raise funds to improve their club's facilities. Under the direction of long-time conductor Mr Jordan Davies, Superintendant at Mount Carmel Chapel in Caerphilly, the choir flourished, beginning a tradition of singing in aid of charities and good causes. During the Depression, for example, a number of choristers toured the south coast of England raising money to ease the suffering of the unemployed and their families back home. During its long history the choir has sung at many prestigious venues in the United Kingdom and made several successful appearances both on television and radio and in competition at various eisteddfodau. A number of popular L.P. recordings of the choir have also been made over the years.

Workmen's Hall and Cinema, Caerphilly, 1973.

The one-time Palace Theatre on the right, behind Castle Street, 1971. Pitt's Palace Theatre was first opened c. 1904 as a roller-skating rink, a popular leisure activity at that time. About 1910 it became a music hall and theatre showing silent films and also hosting boxing bouts. In 1921 the theatre seems to have ceased business faced as it was with competition from the Castle Cinema and the Caerphilly Workmen's Hall. After the Second World War the now semi-derelict building was acquired by Ryans to warehouse their vehicles and finally in 1976 the site was cleared by W.T. Davies (Transport) Ltd of Cardiff.

The fair in Caerphilly.

The Bowls Inn, Penyrheol, 1930s.

Three eminent historians of Caerphilly together with the then Chairman of Caerphilly Urban District Council, Cllr. Douglas Thomas, 1971. From left to right, Henry Simons, H.P. Richards and William Rees.

Twelve
Sport

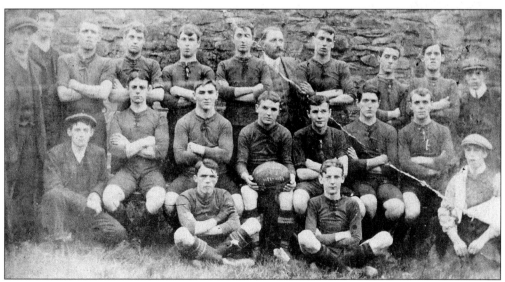

Llanbradach Harlequins rugby team, 1910–11 season.

Caerphilly Cricket XI, *c.* 1912.

Llanbradach Bowls Club, 1936. Among those pictured are Llew Dowling, Harold Palmer, Gavin Palmer, Emlyn Davies, Hughie Jones, Harold Wise, Rod Davies, Reuben Evans, Tom Head, Edmund John, Les Coppage, Bill John.

Caerphilly Grammar Technical School cricket 1st XI, 1954. From left to right, back row: George Morgan, ? Williams, Keith Thomas, Brian Smith, Graham Evans, Bobby Jones, Colin Stenner, Lyndon Peters. Front row: Mr Richard Bell Jones (head teacher), Winford Davies, Paul Bassett, Peter Gatehouse, Owen Williams, John Srodzinski, Mr Reuben Baillieux (sports master).

Windsor Colliery cricket team, Abertridwr, winners of the Rhymney Valley Cup, 1955.

Caerphilly Grammar Technical School cricket team, 1961. Standing, from left to right: Clive Ashcroft, John Turkey, Mike Morgan, 'Joe' Baker, -?-, Roger Williams. Sitting: Mr R. Bell-Jones, Ceri Thomas, Malcolm Bull, David Blake, Basil Turner, Nigel Burnett, Mr 'Rowly' Parsons.

Llanbradach football club, 1954. From left to right, back row: Billy Tilley, Ronnie Hurn, Keith Butler, Freddie Ballinger, Gerald Kearle, Bryn Jones, Derek Hawthorn. Front row: R. Smart, John Srodzinski, Jimmy Hudd, Sammy Gater.

Senghenydd rugby sevens team, 1963–64 season. From left to right, back row: Gary Rees, Mervyn John, Mike Morgan, Gwilym Davies. Front row: Tony Petrie, Keith Thomas, Dai Roberts.

Caerphilly Ladies hockey team, *c.* 1963. The "likely lads" they played were from BNS (British Nylon Spinners) in Pontypool.

Caerphilly Golf Club, c. 1905. The driving force behind the creation of a golf course in Caerphilly was Mr Charlie Goodfellow who had been captivated by the game while holidaying in Minehead. The official formation of the club took place in 1905 and the founder members, in addition to Mr Goodfellow were: Alderman J.E. Evans, Alderman W.H. Renwick, Mr J.H. Phillips, Mr W.A. Phillips and Mr Maurice Harris. A Mr Fernie, a Penarth professional, was commissioned to design and lay out nine holes on the land of Pencapel Farm and Plas Watford, and the area occupied by the course remained substantially the same until 1963.

Members at Caerphilly Golf Club, 1930s.

President, officers and executive committee members during the Golden Jubilee year (1906–1956) of Caerphilly Golf Club.

Club officers, participants and guests on the occasion of the exhibition match organised to celebrate the opening of the present 4th, 5th and 17th holes, 22 June 1963.

Wedding of Les Coppage and Gladys Moore, outside the vicarage of All Saints' Church, Llanbradach, 27 February 1922.

Acknowledgements

I would like to thank all those members of Caerphilly Local History Society who have helped in the compilation of the book, in particular Mr Dennis Sellwood, Mrs Joan Carmichael and Mrs Briony Srodzinski, whose kindness and generosity has been much appreciated. During the course of my researches I was also delighted to work with Mr Glyndwr G. Jones, who lent many pictures and much information for publication. Without his efforts and enthusiastic assistance the book would have been much the poorer.

A grateful mention must also be made of two photographers: Francis William Gatehouse and Victor Corelli Hardacre, both of whom were extremely active in chronicling Caerphilly and the surrounding district, and have thus made an invaluable contribution to the study of the area's historical development during the twentieth century. Several of their photographs appear in the pages of this book.

Special thanks also go to: Mr Jeff Carter; Mrs D. Clapham; John Coppage; Peter Gatehouse; Brian Geen; Margaret Griffiths and Mid-Glamorgan County Libraries; A.A.W.(Tony) Goodman; Miss Betty Holroyd; Miss Kitty Hughes; Mrs Beryl James; Marjorie Jones; Alan Morgan; Vilma and Michael Morgan; John Owen; John Poole; Mrs Joan Powell; the members of Seion Baptist Church, Llanbradach; Edward J. Starr; Mr & Mrs John Williams.

Finally, I wish to apologise for any omissions or errors, for which I am wholly responsible. May I also take this opportunity to invite those readers with different or better images of Caerphilly's past to join the individuals listed above in allowing the local history society to copy your photographs and postcards and thereby preserve our heritage.